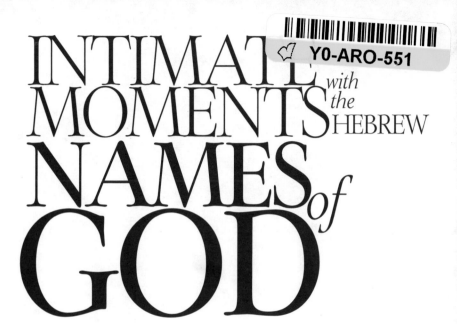

INTIMATE MOMENTS
NAMES
with *the* HEBREW
NAMES *of*
GOD

INTIMATE MOMENTS *with the* HEBREW

NAMES *of* GOD

Barri Cae Mallin & Shmuel Wolkenfeld

ברוך השם

Bridge-Logos *Publishers*

Gainesville, Florida 32614 USA

Scripture quotations in the Appendix are from the Holy Bible: New International Version. Copyright © 1973, 1978, 1984 by the International Bible Society. Used by permission of Zondervan Bible Publishers.

INTIMATE MOMENTS WITH THE HEBREW NAMES OF GOD
by Barri Cae Mallin & Shmuel Wolkenfeld
Copyright © 1999 by Bridge-Logos Publishers
Library of Congress Catalog Card Number: 99-69628
International Standard Book Number: 0-88270-801-5
Reprint 2001

Published by:
Bridge-Logos *Publishers*
Gainesville, FL 32614
http://www.bridgelogos.com

Bibliography

The Holy Bible, New King James Version
Thomas Nelson Publishers, Nashville, TN, 1985.

The Holy Scriptures
Koren Publishers, Jerusalem, Israel, 1997.

The New Testament in Hebrew and English
The Society for Distributing Hebrew Scriptures, Edgware,
Middlesex, England, 1993.

The Quest Study Bible, New International Version
Zondervan Publishing House, Grand Rapids, MI, 1994.

Acknowledgments

Thank you to Bridge-Logos Publishers, who God blessed me to bring this work to publication; to Shmuel Wolkenfeld, who selflessly gave of his time to check every word, verse and phrase; to Pastor Richard Wurmbrand, who continues to speak volumes into my life through his life's example; and to Yeshua HaMaschiach, Jesus the Messiah, my LORD, Savior, my Adonai.

Preface

This book was birthed just a few months ago, before the most challenging time of my life. It seems as though we can experience joy at times of sorrow; we also experience sorrow during times of great joy. Valley experiences occur throughout Scripture; often the greatest growth of one's life occurs during the low times of life. This devotional came about at that time in my life.

In May 1999, the company with whom I was employed decided to relocate me to Kansas City. Kansas City is my original home. However, after coming to faith in Jesus in 1980, in Dallas, God gave me opportunities to establish 'new' families within the Body of the Messiah in all of the cities in which I had lived. Being always single, my life was transient. I was transferred to Nashville, Tennessee, in March 1995. I loved the city of

Nashville; it was small but offered wonderful events. I loved the congregations in which I served; it was the first place I ever put down roots, never expecting to leave.

So when notice of my relocation came, I was very sad, knowing that the Lord was calling me to a different place—perhaps an uncomfortable place, but a place where I was going to need Him more than ever. Then, during vacation in early July, I mis-stepped and broke my foot. Healing did not occur and surgery was required one month later. Recuperation required me to remain horizontal, as healing required the foot to be elevated above the heart. For an active employee, marathoner and worship dancer, this was the antithesis of my life. I found myself reading anything and everything I could on surrender and absolute abandonment to Jesus. I also read about martyrs for Jesus—all this brought me comfort.

In the midst of this time, the Lord impressed upon my heart to be His scribe. He also impressed me with Psalms 8, How Majestic is Your Name!

Being raised in a Jewish home, the name of Jesus was never

spoken. However, when God took the veil from my eyes in 1980, and allowed me to 'see' the truth about Jesus, His name became the most beloved name to me. This Jewish woman loves to sing those hymns about His name—"Jesus, Jesus, There's Just Something About That Name!"

Through those nine weeks, during my daily devotionals, God sweetly brought Scripture verses into my heart—verses that honored His name. Most of these verses are in the Old Testament; some are in the New Testament. It was important to write all those names in the original language—Hebrew. The *Jerusalem Bible Masoretic Text* was my source.

William Cowper's hymn states: "God works in mysterious ways, His wonders to perform. Faith tells me that we who know Him will always win, but will the victory be ours on this side?"

I shall not try to understand the meaning of the trials, or the reasons for the anvil of affliction. Yet, in the midst of the affliction, Lord, help me to see something beautiful come from the blows of Your hand, knowing that the blows are given in love.

INTIMATE MOMENTS

I thank You for the privilege of being Your scribe and Your child, and I can only pray that Your fragrance will come forth from the reading of this text. How I love Your name, Yeshua HaMashiach, Jesus the Messiah. Amen.

Barri Cae Mallin
November 1999

ADONAI

A-do-ni

Let them know that You, whose Name is the LORD—that You alone are the Most High over all the earth.

Psalm 83:18, NIV

This name, A-do-ni, LORD is too sacred to even pronounce as it really is. Lord, Your name is all I need in this life to get by. I don't need wealth, fame, power—all I need is You. You give me the fulfillment within that nothing else will ever satisfy. How beautiful is Your Name. Thank You that Your holy language is sacred. Your name is sacred. How I praise You for this knowledge. May I honor Your life in me, as I journey onward, desiring to do Your will. Blessed is the Name.

ALMIGHTY

Sha-di

He who dwells in the shelter of the Most High will rest in the shadow of the Almighty.

Psalm 91:1, NIV

How I praise You, El Sha-di, Almighty, maker of heaven and earth! There is peace in my soul when I come into Your secret place. There is no other place that I would rather be than under Your shadow. Thank You for Your ever-present protection.

AMEN

Ah-mayn

These are the words of the Amen, the faithful and true witness, the ruler of God's creation.

Revelation 3:14, NIV

You are the Beginning and the End,
You are the Amen.
Thank You that whatever my need is—that You are the Amen.

I have a need—God is the Amen.
I have a hurt—God is the Amen.
I have an illness—God is the Amen.
I lack—God is the Amen.

I need no other answer—Your Word is the best one yet!
You said it, I believe it. That settles it. Amen.

*Like Your name, O God, Your praise reaches to the ends of the earth;
Your right hand is filled with righteousness.* Psalm 48:10

ANCIENT OF DAYS

עתיק יומין

Ah-teek Yo-meen

"As I looked, thrones were set in place, and the Ancient of Days took his seat. His clothing was as white as snow; the hair of his head was white like wool."

Daniel 7:9, NIV

8

From before time was, You Are. Father, to know that You are the Ancient of Days, the Ahteek Yo-meen, gives me great peace and assurance for the days ahead. Thank You for this shalom, this peace.

THE ANGEL OF HIS PRESENCE

מלאך פניו

Mal-akh Pah-nav

*In all their distress He too was distressed,
and the angel of His presence saved them.*

Isaiah 63:9, NIV

10

Thank You, Father, for the Angel of Your Presence that is there always to protect me. May I never stray from Your ever-watchful eye. Thank You for all of the dangers from which You have protected me, many of which I shall never be aware. How I praise the Mal-akh Pah-nav.

I will praise You forever for what You have done; in Your name I will hope, for Your name is good. I will praise You in the presence of Your saints. (Psalm 52:9)

BREAD OF LIFE

Leh-khem Khi-yeem

"I am the bread of life."

John 6:48, NIV

Born in Beit Lechem (House of Bread), You give life to all who come to You. Lord, how blessed I am to know You, the Bread of Life, Leh-khem Khi-yeem—and to know that I will never hunger again.

CAPSTONE

ראש פנה

Rosh Pee-nah

The stone the builders rejected has become the capstone; the LORD has done this, and it is marvelous in our eyes.

Psalm 118:22-23, NIV

14

Father,

Thank You that when everything around me looks like shifting sand, I have the assurance of the Rosh Pee-nah, the Capstone. Messiah Yeshua is that Capstone, on which my faith is built. Thank You for His example, and thank You for the help that You give that enables me to follow Him.

Now, our God, we give You thanks, and praise Your glorious name. (1 Chronicles 29:13)

COUNSELOR

Yo-ayts

For unto us a child is born, to us a son is given, and the government will be on His shoulders. And He will be called . . .Counselor. . .

Isaiah 9:6, NIV

16

Dear Father,

Your counsel rules over all earthly machinations. You are Sovereign, and I am so thankful that I can come to You for the best counsel. Thank You for this wisdom from above—from You. Help me to have ears to hear, and a heart ready to accept. I thank You for being the Best Counselor—Yo-ayts.

CREATOR

בּוֹרֵא

Boh-ray

Do you not know? Have you not heard? The LORD is the everlasting God the Creator of the ends of the earth. He will not grow tired or weary, and His understanding no one can fathom.

Isaiah 40:28, NIV

It boggles my mind to think that You, the Creator—Boh-ray—of the universe, know me. May I live my life in thankfulness for all that You have done, are doing and will do in my life. How I praise Your name!

I called on Your name, O LORD, from the depths of the pit. (Lamentations 3:55)

ETERNAL GOD

אלהי קדם

Eh-lo-hay Keh-dem

*The eternal God is your refuge, and underneath are
the everlasting arms.*

Deuteronomy 33:27, NIV

20

Eternal God, Eh-lo-hay Keh-dem, You know my beginning and my end. How my soul is at peace. Thank You for this timeless truth. Thank You that I can trust my life with You; what total peace this gives my soul. I love you and I thank You for loving me.

May His name endure forever; may it continue as long as the sun. (Psalm 72:17)

ETERNAL KING

מלך עולם

Meh-lekh O-lahm

*But the LORD is the true God; He is the living God,
the eternal King.*

Jeremiah 10:10, NIV

You are the Everlasting King. Before time began, You reigned. You reign today. You will reign forevermore. Meh-lekh O-lahm, Eternal King, I praise You. What assurance and peace this truth is, that no matter what assails me, Your power will ultimately conquer. Thank You for this perfect divine plan.

EVERLASTING FATHER

עד אבי

Ah-vee Ahd

For to us a child is born, to us a son is given, and the government will be on his shoulders. And he will be called . . .
Everlasting Father . . .

Isaiah 9:6, NIV

24

The same Father who led our father Abraham is the same Father who leads me. This is almost too overwhelming to understand. Yet what a comfort it is to know that You, Everlasting Father, Ah-vee Ahd, lead me too.

EVERLASTING GOD

El Olahm

Then Abraham planted a tamarisk tree in Beersheva, and there called on the name of the LORD, the Everlasting God.

Genesis 21:33, NKJV

You were there at my birth; You will be there at my death. Thank You, Lord, that You even recorded Abraham's planting of a tree. Thank You that even the smallest thing done in Your name will not go unnoticed by You. How I praise You, my Everlasting God—El Olahm.

From the rising of the sun to the place where it sets, the name of the LORD is to be praised. (Psalm 113:3)

FATHER

אבי

Ah-vee

He will call out to me, 'You are my Father, my God, the Rock my Savior.'

Psalm 89:26, NIV

28

There is nothing else more comforting to me, than to know that You are my Father, Ah-vee. Thank You for the miraculous ways that You provide for me. Thank You for the many ways that You shower me with Father-love. Please forgive me for my childish outbursts, for deep down, I know that You, Father—Ah-vee—know best.

Let them praise His name with dancing and make music to Him with tambourine and harp. (Psalm 149:3)

29

FATHER OF THE HEAVENLY LIGHTS

אבי   המארת

Ah-vee Ha-M'o-rot

Every good and perfect gift is from above, coming down from the Father of the heavenly lights, who does not change like shifting shadows.

James 1:17, NIV

Every good thing that happens in my life is from You. Thank You, dear Ah-vee Ha-M'o-rot, Father of the heavenly lights. Even in the trials, You bring forth good. Thank You that You are never-changing, always loving. There is no variation. You are the same yesterday, today and forever. Thank You for giving light to my path.

GOD MOST HIGH

אלהים עליון

Eh-lo-heem El-yon

I cry out to God Most High, to God, who fulfills His purpose for me.

Psalm 57:2, NIV

I cry out to You, for You hear me and Your ear is not deaf to my cry. O God, You know my heart cry, and only You can fill that empty place inside. By faith, I will wait for Your hand of deliverance, Eh-lo-heem El-yon.

He restores my soul. He guides me in paths of righteousness for His name's sake. (Psalm 23:3)

GOD OF ALL COMFORT

אלהי כל נחמה

Eh-lo-hay Khawl Na-kha-mah

Praise be to the God and Father of our Lord Jesus Christ (Yeshua HaMashiach), the Father of compassion and the God of all comfort.

2 Corinthians 1:3, NIV

34

What a comfort to know You, the God of all comfort. No matter what my affliction, Your comfort is greater. Thank You that in the midst of a storm, You are my peace, my Shalom, oh God of all comfort, Eh-lo-hay khawl Na-kha-mah.

I will give thanks to the LORD because of His righteousness and will sing praise to the name of the LORD Most High. (Psalm 7:17)

GOD OF ALL GRACE

אלהי החסד

Eh-lo-hay Ha-Khe-sed

And the God of all grace, who called you to his eternal glory in Christ (Mashiach), after you have suffered a little while, will Himself restore you and make you strong, firm and steadfast.

1 Peter 5:10, NIV

Dear God,

I know that You are waiting for me at the finish line of this trial. As I persevere, thank You for perfecting and establishing me in Messiah. Thank You, Eh-lo-hay Ha-Khe-sed, for always bringing me through victoriously. Thank You that success is not dependent on my strength, but my reliance of Your strength and Your grace. How lovely is Your name, O God of all grace.

In that day you will say: "Give thanks to the LORD, call upon His name; make known among the nations what He has done, and proclaim that His name is exalted." (Isaiah 12:4)

GOD OF ALL MANKIND

אלהי כל בשר

Eh-lo-hay Kawl Bah-sar

"I am the LORD, the God of all mankind. Is anything too hard for Me?"

Jeremiah 32:27, NIV

38

How I praise You! Oh Eh-lo-hay Kawl Bah-sar, Thank You that there are no limits to You. We are but flesh, but You reign over all flesh. How I praise You for Your wonderful creation. Thank You for Yeshua, Jesus, who came as God in the flesh, to show me how to live. Words cannot describe my joy in thanksgiving to You!

GOD OF ALL THE EARTH

אלהי כל הארץ

Eh-lo-hay Khawl Ha-Arets

For your Maker is your husband—the LORD Almighty is his name—the Holy One of Israel is your Redeemer; he is called the God of all the earth.

Isaiah 54:5, NIV

How awesome it is for me to think that You, the God of the whole earth, loves me. You, Eh-lo-hay Khawl Ha-Arets, care for the birds, the animals, and me. How I praise Your name, for You alone are great.

GOD OF HOSTS

אלהים צבאֹת

Eh-lo-heem Ts'va-ot

Restore us, O God of Hosts; Cause Your face to shine, and we shall be saved.

Psalm 80:7, NKJV

42

O God of hosts, Eh-lo-heem Ts'va-ot, God of the Armies of Heaven. Thank You that the power of Your might goes before me in battle. You surround me with the Hosts of Heaven and Armies of Heaven to help me. Thank You that as I yield myself to You, Your strength is around me. Help me to go through the day ever aware that You, the God of Hosts, the God of the Armies of Heaven, are with me.

GOD OF ISRAEL

אלהי ישראל

Eh-lo-hay Yis-ra-el

*The people were amazed when they saw the mute
speaking, the crippled made well, the lame walking
and the blind seeing. And they praised the God of Israel.*

Matthew 15:31, NIV

44

You, the God of Israel, Eh-lo-hay Yis-ra-el, are the same yesterday, today and forever. Thank You for Your divine guidance in my life, O God of Israel. He that keeps Israel (and me) never slumbers or sleeps. What a comfort You are.

I will sacrifice a freewill offering to You; I will praise Your name, O LORD, for it is good. (Psalm 54:6)

GOD OF JACOB

אלהי

יעקב

Eh-lo-hay Yah-ah-kov

May the LORD answer you when you are in distress;
may the name of the God of Jacob protect you.

Psalm 20:1, NIV

There is only One who knows my thoughts, who hears my heart, who can answer my prayers. The same God who led Jacob is the same God who leads me. There is much comfort in knowing You, Eh-lo-hay Yah-ah-kov.

GOD OF LOVE AND PEACE

אלהי

האהבה והשלום

Eh-lo-hay Ha-ah-ha-vah V'ha-sha-lom

Finally, brothers, good-by. Aim for perfection, listen to my appeal, be of one mind, live in peace. And the God of love and peace will be with you.

2 Corinthians 13:11, NIV

Love and peace—two wonderful attributes of You, Lord. Thank You! Thank You that Your love is not dependent upon my right deeds or my right living, but it is based on You and Your love for me. How I praise Your name, Eh-lo-hay Ha-ah-ha-vah V'ha-sha-lom.

GOD OF MY FATHER

אלהי

אבי

Eh-lo-hay Ah-vee

*"I see that your father's attitude toward me is not
what it was before, but the God of my father has
been with me."*
Genesis 31:5, NIV

How grateful I am for the assurance of Your presence with me. I need not worry about the future, or others' opinions of me, for I know that You will be with me. Thank You, Eh-lo-hay Ah-vee, the God of my father.

Through You we push back our enemies; through Your name we trample our foes.
(Psalm 44:5)

GOD OF MY PRAISE

אלהי תהלתי

Eh-lo-hay T'hee-lah-tee

Do not keep silent, O God of my praise.

Psalm 109:1, NKJV

52

O God, how I praise You for the answers that You give to my prayers. Sometimes, yes, there is silence and I want to ask why. At these times, help me to hang on to Your every promise, and help me believe in my heart that You will never leave me, You will never forsake me, and You will answer my prayers. I will wait on You, Eh-lo-hay T'hee-lah-tee.

Yes, LORD, walking in the way of Your laws, we wait for You; Your name and renown are the desire of our hearts. (Isaiah 26:8)

GOD OF MY RIGHTEOUSNESS

אלהי צדקי

Eh-lo-hay Tseed-kee

Hear me when I call, O God of my righteousness! You have relieved me in my distress; have mercy on me, and hear my prayer.

Psalm 4:1, NKJV

54

O God, my righteousness is all because of Yeshua, Jesus, living in my heart. Messiah in me, the Hope of Glory, is the praise on my mouth today. For God made Messiah who knew no sin, to be sin for us, that we might become the righteousness of God, in Messiah. O Eh-lo-hay Tseed-kee, how I praise You for the bounty of blessings You give!

GOD OF PEACE

אלהי השלום

Eh-lo-hay Ha-Sha-lom

The God of peace will soon crush Satan under your feet.

Romans 16:20, NIV

56

You are the God of Peace, Eh-lo-hay Ha-Sha-lom. Yet I thank You because You go to battle for me. How glad I am that I need not trust in my hands, my ability or my strength for defense. I simply put my life into Your hands and have all the help I need. How I praise You!

GOD, THE LORD, THE STRENGTH OF MY SALVATION

יהוה אדני
עז ישועתי

A-do-ni A-do-ni Oz Y'shu-a-tee

*O GOD, the Lord, the strength of my salvation,
You have covered my head in the day of battle.*

Psalm 140:7, NKJV

O Lord, You give me the strength to work out
my own salvation, with fear and trembling. I
look to You for help. Some days seem so hard,
but all You ask me to do is to rest in You for
You are the strength of my salvation, A-do-ni
A-do-ni Oz Y'shu-a-tee. Thank You for Your help,
Your hand of deliverance.

GOD WHO FORGIVES

אל נשא

El No-say

You answered them, O LORD our God;
You were to them God-who-forgives.

Psalm 99:8, NKJV

60

O LORD, how many times a day are You God-who-forgives. How I thank You for Your never-failing love, your loving kindness, O El No-say, God-who-forgives. May I live this day with a humble heart, knowing that my goodness is not of me, but of Thee; my sinfulness is of me but because of Thee, I am forgiven.

Turn to me and have mercy on me, as You always do to those who love Your name. (Psalm 119:132)

GOD WHO SAVES ME

אלהי תשועתי

Eh-lo-hay T'shu-a-tee

Save me from bloodguilt, O God, the God who saves me, and my tongue will sing of your righteousness.

Psalm 51:14, NIV

62

In thought, word or deed, I have erred in Your sight; and I thank you that You are the God of my salvation, Eh-lo-hay T'shu-a-tee. Thank You for the Blood of the Lamb that cleanses me from all my sins, and allows me access to Your throne of grace.

O LORD, You are my God; I will exalt You and praise Your name, for in perfect faithfulness You have done marvelous things, things planned long ago. (Isaiah 25:1)

GUIDE OF MY YOUTH

אלוף נערי

Ah-loof N'Oo-ri

"Will you not from this time cry to Me,
'My Father, You are to me the Guide of my youth'?"

Jeremiah 3:4, NKJV

64

When my heart is overwhelmed and I have no where else to go, I run to You, Ah-loof N'Oo-ri, Guide of my Youth. You know my ways; You will lead me on level paths. How I praise Your name!

For Your name's sake, O LORD, preserve my life; in Your righteousness, bring me out of trouble. (Psalm 143:11)

HOLY

Ka-dosh

For this is what the high and lofty One says—He who lives forever, whose name is Holy;

Isaiah 57:15, NIV

Holy is Your name; Holiness befits You. Thank You that it is not on my merit that I can approach You, but it is because of the shed Blood of Yeshua, Jesus, that I can approach Your throne of grace, and have the privilege to call you Holy—Ka-dosh.

All the earth bows down to You; they sing praise to You, they sing praise to Your name. (Psalm 66:4)

HOLY ONE OF ISRAEL

קדוש ישראל

Ka-dosh Yis-ra-el

*For I am the LORD, your God, the Holy One of Israel,
your Savior . . .*

Isaiah 43:3, NIV

Father, may I never be put in a position to tempt You, Ka-dosh Yis-ra-el, Holy One of Israel. May I only seek to do Your will. You are Holy and I cannot look upon You, except by the Blood of the Sinless Seh ha-Elohim, the Lamb of God. What a gift You have given, O Holy One of Israel.

Glory in His holy name; let the hearts of those who seek the LORD rejoice. (1 Chronicles 16:10)

HOPE OF ISRAEL

מקוה ישראל

Meek-vay Yis-ra-el

*O LORD, the hope of Israel, all who forsake
you will be put to shame.*

Jeremiah 17:13, NIV

70

You are my Hope, O Meek-vay Yis-ra-el. My sorrow may endure for the evening but joy comes in the morning. You are my Hope; when all else fails, there is You. Help me never to give up on Your Wonderful Name.

HORN OF SALVATION

קרן ישעי

Keh-ren Yeesh-ee

The LORD is my rock, my fortress, and my deliverer; my God is my rock, in whom I take refuge. He is my shield and the horn of my salvation.

Psalm 18:2, NIV

72

As the priest would grab onto the horns of the altar when he prayed, I grab onto You, Ke-hren Yeesh-ee, the Horn of Salvation. You are my help, my Deliverer, You give me liberty, and favor. Thank You that You have my best interests at heart. How I love Your name.

Surely the righteous will praise Your name and the upright will live before You. (Psalm 140:13)

I AM WHO I AM

אהיה
אשר אהיה

Eh-yeh Ah-sher Eh-yeh

*God said to Moses, "I AM WHO I AM. This is what you are to say
to the Israelites: I AM has sent me to you."*

Exodus 3:14, NIV

74

You are timeless. How grateful I am to know that You hold all of the keys to the Kingdom. Today I rest in knowing You, the Great I AM, Eh-yeh Ah-sher Eh-yeh. You are the same— yesterday, today, and forever. What peace that brings to my soul.

IMMANUEL

עמנו·אל

Ee-ma-noo-el

Therefore the Lord himself will give you a sign:
The virgin will be with child and will give birth to a
son, and will call him Immanuel.

Isaiah 7:14, NIV

76

Immanuel—God with us.
God, You never forsake us.
God, You never are not with us.
Thank You for Your marvelous plan, and that I
can always know Immanuel—God with us.

*But let all who take refuge in You be glad; let
them ever sing for joy. Spread Your protection
over them, that those who love Your name may
rejoice in You.* (Psalm 5:11)

JACOB'S KING

מלך
יעק ב

Meh-lekh Ya-a-cov

"Present your case," says the LORD.
"Set forth your arguments," says Jacob's King.

Isaiah 41:21, NIV

What a call to prayer! Father, I beseech You, O Holy One, grow me up into Messiah-likeness. As I wait for You to bring forth the desires of my heart, O Meh-lekh Ya-a-cov, my number one prayer request is to reveal to my loved ones who You are. May my family table be filled at the Marriage Supper of the Lamb, O Jacob's King.

JEALOUS

Kah-nah

Do not worship any other god, for the LORD,
whose name is Jealous, is a jealous God.

Exodus 34:14, NIV

Father,

Help me to discipline my eyes and my whole being to desire no other gods but You. I desire to worship the Creator, not the creature. There is no other name but Yours, Kah-nah, Jealous God.

JUDGE

שפט

Sho-fayt

And the heavens proclaim his righteousness,
for God himself is judge.

Psalm 50:6, NIV

Father,

Thank You that You do not give me what I so often deserve. But because of the Blood of Yeshua, You give me so much more. Thank You, Sho-fayt, Judge. Thank You for Your perfect judgment.

I will be glad and rejoice in You, I will sing praise to Your name, O Most High. (Psalm 9:2)

KING

מלך

Meh-lekh

*The LORD is King for ever and ever; the nations
will perish from his land.*

Psalm 10:16, NIV

84

It is good to know that there is no other king higher than our Meh-lekh, our King. In the daily battles of life, if we know the King, we will have victory.

O Lord, how I thank You that I need to never worry about the battles in my life, for You will gain the victory. How blessed I am to be a King's kid!

KING ETERNAL

מלך עולם

Meh-lekh O-lahm

Now to the King eternal, immortal, invisible, the only God, be honor and glory for ever and ever. Amen.

1 Timothy 1:17, NIV

How thankful I am to know You, King Eternal, Meh-lekh O-lahm. Even though You are invisible, You are nearer to me than my own breath. May I live this day in total thankfulness. May I live this day with a sense of Your closeness. I love You, dear Lord.

And everyone who calls on the name of the LORD will be saved. (Joel 2:32)

KING OF GLORY

מלך

הכבוד

Meh-lekh Ha-Ka-vod

Lift up your heads, O you gates; be lifted up, you ancient doors,
that the King of glory may come in. Who is this King of glory?
The LORD strong and mighty, the LORD mighty in battle.

Psalm 24:7-8, NIV

You are the King of glory, the Me-lekh Ha-Ka-vod. The King of Royal Esteem, Majesty and Abundance. Lord, how I thank You for the Glory, the Kavod of Your Name. May I so live as to bring honor to the King.

Glorify the LORD with me; let us exalt His name together. (Psalm 34:3)

KING OF KINGS

מלך המלכים

Meh-lekh Ha-M'lah-kheem

On His robe and on His thigh He has this name
written: KING OF KINGS AND LORD OF LORDS.

Revelation 19:16, NIV

90

That You are the King of all the kings who ever was, are or ever will be, is sometimes too much for me to fully comprehend. But I am thankful to be Your child. Thank You for the imperishable inheritance that awaits me from the Meh-lekh Ha-M'lah-kheem, the KING OF KINGS.

KING OF THE NATIONS

מלך הגוים

Meh-lekh Ha Goy-yeem

Who should not revere You, O King of the nations? This is Your due, Among all the wise men of the nations and in all the kingdoms, there is no one like You.

Jeremiah 10:7, NIV

King of the nations, Meh-lekh Ha Goy-yeem, how I praise Your name, for there is none like You. Others may try to usurp Your kingly reign, but they are fools in Your sight. Thank You that no matter where I am, You are King.

LAMB OF GOD

שה האלהים

Seh Ha-Eh-lo-heem

*"Look, the Lamb of God, who takes away the
sin of the world!"*

John 1:29, NIV

94

O LORD, You are the Pure, Sinless Lamb of God, Seh Ha-Eh-lo-heem. You laid down Your life to redeem my life from the curse of the enemy, once and for all. How I praise You, Lamb of God!

Praise the LORD, O my soul; all my inmost being, praise His holy name. (Psalm 103:1)

LIGHT OF ISRAEL

אוֹר יִשְׂרָאֵל

Or Yis-rah-el

The Light of Israel will become a fire, their Holy One a flame; . . .

Isaiah 10:17, NIV

You are the Light of Israel and the Light of the world. You set the heavens in orbit. You chose Jerusalem as Your holy city. Light of Israel, Or Yis-rah-el, shine forth. Shine Your light into our darkness, O Light of Israel.

LIGHT OF THE WORLD

אור העולם

Or Ha-O-lahm

"I am the light of the world. Whoever follows me will never walk in darkness, but will have the light of life."

John 8:12, NIV

98

O Lord, there is none like You. You are the light of the world. You are not selective. You give Your light to all who desire to know You. Thank You for shining Your light into my world and into my life. Thank You, Or Ha-O-lahm, for changing my attitude, my thoughts, and my life—from darkness to light.

Blessed be Your glorious name, and may it be exalted above all blessing and praise. (Nehemiah 9:5)

LIVING GOD

אל חי

El Khi

My soul yearns, even faints, for the courts of the LORD;
my heart and my flesh cry out for the living God.

Psalm 84:2, NIV

100

O LORD, there are inexpressible yearnings within my heart, and You know them all. Only You satisfy, El Khi, Living God. My soul longs for You and I desire Your closeness and Your comfort. O Living God, how I love You.

We give thanks to You, O God, we give thanks, for Your name is near; men tell of Your wonderful deeds. (Psalm 75:1)

LORD

A-do-ni YHVH

*I appeared to Abraham, to Isaac, and to Jacob as God Almighty,
but by my name the LORD I did not make Myself known to them.*

Exodus 6:3, NIV

102

For all of my loved ones who don't know You personally, will You reveal Yourself to them? O Lord, YHVH, A-do-ni, please reveal who You are to them, for knowing You is the greatest joy of my life. I trust You.

LORD GOD

יהוה אלהים

A-do-ni Eh-lo-heem

When the LORD God made the earth and the heavens—and no shrub of the field had yet appeared on the earth and no plant of the field had yet sprung up, for the LORD God had not sent rain on the earth and there was no man to work the ground, but streams came up from the earth and watered the whole surface of the ground—

Hebrew Names of God

the LORD God formed man from the dust of the ground and breathed into his nostrils the breath of life, and the man became a living being.

Genesis 2:4-7, NIV

Just as You made the earth and the heavens, Lord God, You made me, too. You formed me from the womb; Your hands made me. A-do-ni Eh-lo-heem, I praise Your wonderful name and Your marvelous works. And You even know what awaits me today. Thank You that I can rest in calm assurance and trust You.

Therefore I will praise You among the nations, O LORD; I will sing praises to Your name. (Psalm 18:49)

LORD GOD OF GODS

יהוה
אל אלהים

A-do-ni Ehl Eh-lo-heem

The LORD God of gods, He knows . . . .

Joshua 22:22, NKJV

106

When I stop to think of all the concerns of others, the major events and needs in the world, how comforted I am to know that You care. Just as You know every sparrow, You know the hairs on my head. Thank You, A-do-ni Ehl Eh-lo-heem, for Your Sovereign love and care for me. How I praise Your Name!

LORD, THE GOD OF HEAVEN

יהוה
אלהי השמים

A-do-ni Eh-lo-hay HaShah-mi-eem

"The LORD, the God of heaven, who brought me out of my father's household and my native land and who spoke to me and promised

me on oath, saying, 'To your offspring I will give this land', He will send His angel before you . . .

Genesis 24:7, NIV

You are LORD over all the earth and heavens. All I need to do is look up and realize that You are. You, A-do-ni Eh-lo-hay HaShah-mi-eem, see everything. As you spoke to Abraham, You still speak today. How I praise You for Your marvelous ways.

He provided redemption for His people; He ordained His covenant forever—holy and awesome is His name. (Psalm 111:9)

LORD, THE GOD OF ISRAEL

יהוה

אלהי ישראל

A-do-ni Eh-lo-hay Yis-rah-el

Joshua said to all the people, "This is what the LORD, the God of Israel, says: 'Long ago your forefathers, including Terah the father of Abraham and Nahor, lived beyond the river and worshiped other gods."

Joshua 24:2, NIV

110

Lord, in these times when other activities and temptations try to steal my love away from You, help me to cling even closer to You. I choose to serve A-do-ni Eh-lo-hay Yis-rah-el, the Lord, the God of Israel. I desire You, O Lord, for only You satisfy the longing in my soul. Thank You for the peace You always give.

LORD, GOD OF OUR FATHERS

יהוה

אלהי אבתינו

A-do-ni Eh-lo-hay Ah-vo-tay-nu

*Praise be to the LORD, the God of our fathers, who has
put it in the king's heart to bring honor to the house
of the LORD in Jerusalem in this way and who has extended*

112

*His good favor to me before the king and his advisers
and all the king's powerful officials.*

Ezra 7:27, NIV

From generation to generation, You reign
supreme over all the earth. What a comfort it is
to know that You are the same God, A-do-ni
Eh-lo-hay Ah-vo-tay-nu. From Abraham to
Moses to David—the patriarchs and I have the
same Lord. How blessed am I.

*Praise be to the name of God for ever and ever;
wisdom and power are His.* (Daniel 2:20)

THE LORD IS MY BANNER

יהוה נסי

A-do-ni Nee-see

Moses built an altar and called it The LORD is my banner.

Exodus 17:15, NIV

114

Father, thank You that in this imperfect world, You are my banner, my Standard. Your perfection is my goal, and I thank You, A-do-ni Nee-see, that I have You to look up to—through it all.

LORD IS ONE

יהוה אחד
ושמו אחד

A-do-ni Eh-khad Oo-Sh'mo Eh-khad

In that day it shall be —"The LORD is One" and His name one.

Zechariah 14:9, NKJV

What a mystery! God my Father; God as Yeshua, who came to show me how to live; God as the Spirit—Ruach HaKodesh, who empowers me to live the godly life. Three as One—what a mystery.

A-do-ni Eh-khad Oo-Sh'mo Eh-khad—The Lord is One, His Name One. Thank You, Lord, that I don't have to understand this with my head to know it in my heart. How marvelous is Your Name!

Your name, O LORD, endures forever, Your renown, O LORD, through all generations. (Psalm 135:13)

THE LORD IS THERE

יהוה שמה

A-do-ni Shah-mah

"And the name of the city from that time on will be:
THE LORD IS THERE."

Ezekiel 48:35, NIV

A-do-ni Shah-mah (The Lord is There)—what a comfort to know that deep in my soul, whatever trouble assails me, You are there with me. Just as You chose Jerusalem to be the city in which You dwelt, You also dwell in the heart of every child of God. How I praise You for Your eternal truths. Even when I doubt Your presence, I trust Your heart and I know that if I am patient, I will always see Your presence. May I never ever doubt that You are always there for me.

LORD MY GOD

יהוה אלהי

A-do-ni Eh-lo-hi

*Then the LORD my God will come, and all the
holy ones with Him.*

Zechariah 14:5, NIV

120

To know You personally and to see You in everything makes life the greatest adventure ever. What a blessing it is to know You, and to know that You know me, and love me, just as I am. A-do-ni Eh-lo-hi, thank You for loving me.

I will praise God's name in song and glorify Him with thanksgiving. (Psalm 69:30)

LORD, MY ROCK

צורי יהוה

A-do-ni Tsu-ree

Praise be to the LORD my Rock, who trains my hands for war.

Psalm 144:1, NIV

122

How blessed am I to know that You are my Rock, and my fortress. You are the One who equips me to do Your work. Thank You that You equip the called—not call the equipped. Today, help me to realize that You have provided for my every need—one step at a time. A-do-ni Tsu-ree, how I thank You!

LORD OF HOSTS

יהוה צבאות

A-do-ni Ts'vah-ot

*"Holy, holy, holy is the LORD of hosts; the whole
earth is filled with His glory!"*

Isaiah 6:3, NKJV

124

Hebrew Names of God

A-do-ni Ts'vah-ot, Lord of Hosts, how glorious
it is to be in Your presence. My heart and my
flesh sing for joy to You for there is none like
You. You, Lord of hosts, Lord of all heavenly
armies and heavenly hosts—You do battle for
me. As the seraphim cry: M'lo khawl ha-oretz,
b'vodo—the whole earth is full of Your glory.
I shall never let the rocks out-praise me. How I
love You, O Lord of hosts!

LORD OF LORDS

אדן האדנים

A-don Ha-A-do-neem

On His robe and on His thigh He has this name written:
KING OF KINGS AND LORD OF LORDS.

Revelation 19:16, NIV

You are the Lord. You are my master. You know me personally. There is no other need that must be fulfilled; You satisfy my every need. A-don Ha-A-do-neem, Lord of Lords, Thank You for being Lord to me. I love You.

I am the LORD; that is My Name! I will not give My glory to another or My praise to idols. (Isaiah 42:8)

LORD OUR GOD

אלהינו יהוה

A-do-ni   Eh-lo-hay-nu

Exalt the LORD our God and worship at his footstool.
He is holy.

Psalm 99:5, NIV

Lord God, how I praise You for this wonderful plan of redemption that You had before time began. Thank You that You made a way where there seemed to be no way. A-do-ni Eh-lo-hay-nu, Lord our God, You did it back then and I thank You that You continue to work like that today. It is a privilege to be Your child.

LORD OUR MAKER

יהוה עשנו

A-do-ni O-say-noo

*Come, let us bow down in worship, let us kneel before
the LORD our Maker.*

Psalm 95:6, NIV

130

How comforting it is to know that You are my Maker. You know me better than I know myself. Your desires for me are higher than my desires for me. A-do-ni O-say-noo, help me to live this day in submission to Your will, for You made me and You will lead me in paths of righteousness, for Your name's sake. Thank You for loving me.

Do not profane My Holy name. (Leviticus 22:32)

THE LORD OUR RIGHTEOUSNESS

יהוה צדקנו

A-do-ni Tseed-kay-nu

In His days Judah will be saved and Israel will live in
safety. This is the name by which He will be called:
The LORD Our Righteousness.

Jeremiah 23:6, NIV

132

A-do-ni Tseed-kay-nu, The Lord our righteousness. May I always remember it is never me, always Thee. In my goodness, it is Thee. How I praise You that I have no goodness apart from You. How I praise You that Your righteousness can be mine. Help me to be obedient to You—in thought, word and deed.

THE LORD WHO HEALS YOU

יהוה רפאך

A-do-ni Rof-eh-kha

He said, "If you listen carefully to the voice of the LORD
your God and do what is right in His eyes, if you pay attention to
His commands and keep all His decrees, I will not bring on you any
of these diseases I brought on the Egyptians, for I am the LORD,
who heals you."

Exodus 15:26, NIV

134

Thank You, Lord, that when I have no where to turn for help for the sinful things that still combat my soul, You are there. Father, temptations assail me daily, yet You are the Lord who heals me. A-do-ni Rof-eh-kha, help me, heal me from things of the past and from things hidden now. Thank You that You do heal.

LORD WHO SANCTIFIES YOU

יהוה מקדשכם

A-do-ni M'Kah-deesh-khem

Surely my Sabbaths you shall keep, for it is a sign between Me and you throughout your generations, that you may know that I am the LORD who sanctifies you.

Exodus 31:13, NKJV

Lord, thank You for helping me to live a life that is set apart. You are the One who sanctifies me; thank You that it is You who brings the change in me. A-do-ni M'Kah-deesh-khem, thank You for always having my best interests as You lead me. Forgive me when I struggle against Your perfect will, and thank You for Your unfailing love towards me.

Those who know Your name will trust in You, for You, LORD, have never forsaken those who seek You. (Psalm 9:10)

THE LORD WILL PROVIDE

יהוה יראה

A-do-ni Yeer-eh

*So Abraham called that place The LORD Will Provide. And to this
day it is said, "On the mountain of the LORD it will be provided."*

Genesis 22:14, NIV

138

Lord, how grateful I am for Your hand of provision. You give and You withhold—all for my best. You call me to obey, not to sacrifice. A-do-ni Yeer-eh, How I praise You for providing beyond what I could hope for, dream of or ask. Sometimes I feel like I am being backed into a corner with no where to go. And that is exactly the time that You always come through for me. How wonderful it is to know You.

Praise be to His glorious name forever; may the whole earth be filled with His glory. (Psalm 72:19)

LORD YOUR GOD

יהוה אלהיך

Ah-do-ni   Eh-lo-heh-kha

I am the LORD your God, who brought you out of Egypt, out of the land of slavery.

Exodus 20:2, NIV

140

How glorious is Your hand of deliverance. I
have much inner assurance just knowing that
You see me, You know me, and You will perfect
that which concerns me. Ah-do-ni Eh-lo-heh-
kha, the LORD your God, thank You
for being sovereign over all of Your children.

MAJESTIC

אדיר

Ah-deer

*O LORD, our Lord, how majestic is Your name
in all the earth!*

Psalm 8:1, NIV

142

When we pray in the name of Yeshua, there is power in His name. The same power that set His Glory—His Kavod—in the heavens, is the same power available to me. How Majestic—Ah-deer—is Your name. I thank You that I know You by name!

Give thanks to the LORD, call on His name; make known among the nations what He has done. Psalm 105:1

MAKER OF ALL THINGS

יוצר הכל

Yo-tsayr Ha-kol

*He who is the Portion of Jacob is not like these,
for He is the Maker of all things.*

Jeremiah 10:16, NIV

144

You, the Maker of all things—Yo-tsayr Ha-kol—
made me. Your hands fashioned me; You
formed me in the womb. Since You created me,
why should I not trust You with everything in
my life? Thank You for giving me shalom—
peace—in the midst of all that goes on within
me. I surrender my life into Your hands, Maker
of all things.

MIGHTY GOD

אל גבור

El Guee-bor

For to us a child is born, to us a son is given, and the government will be on his shoulders. And He will be called Wonderful Counselor, Mighty God . . . .

Isaiah 9:6, NIV

146

You are the Mighty One, the Champion—El Guee-bor—the Valiant One. How I praise You that when I am weak, then You are strong. There is nothing else I need other than the knowledge that You know me and You love me. What confidence You give to me: the assurance that You go before me in all that I do. Thank You, Lord.

O great and powerful God, whose name is the LORD Almighty, great are Your purposes and mighty are Your deeds. (Jeremiah 32:18-19)

MOST HIGH

El-yon

I will praise You, O LORD, with all my heart;
I will tell of all Your wonders. I will be glad and rejoice in You.
I will sing praise to Your name, O MOST HIGH.

Psalm 9:1-2, NIV

O MOST HIGH—El-yon—Your Omnipotence! You are all-powerful. You are higher than all others in heaven and on earth. Thank You Lord for going to battle for me. You turn back my enemies. I shall not trust in my abilities; I trust in You, O MOST HIGH!

MY BELOVED

Doh-dee

*Now let me sing to my well-beloved a song
of My Beloved regarding His vineyard.*

Isaiah 5:1, NKJV

150

There is no one closer to me but Thee. And besides Thee, my Beloved—Doh-dee—I desire no one else. You are my Beloved and I desire to be true to You all of my life. And yet, what is more is that You look upon me and call me beloved. Thank You for Your boundless, infinite love.

Our Father in heaven, hallowed be Your name. (Matthew 6:9)

MY GOD OF MERCY

אלהי חסדי

Eh-lo-hay Khahs-dee

*My God of mercy shall come to meet me; God shall
let me see my desire on my enemies.*

Psalm 59:10, NKJV

Thank You that You are my God of mercy, Eh-lo-hay Khahs-dee. You surround me with lovingkindness all the days of my life. Thank You for the mercy that You give to Your children; how measureless is Your love. Help me today to be a vessel of Your love and mercy, in gratitude for all that You have done for me.

You shall not misuse the name of the LORD your God, for the LORD will not hold anyone guiltless who misuses His name. (Deuteronomy 5:11)

ONE

אחד

Eh-khahd

And the LORD shall be king over all the earth;
on that day, the LORD shall be One and His name One.

Zechariah 14:9, NKJV

154

Hear O Israel, the Lord, our God, is ONE. He is Eh-khahd. How glorious is that word—Eh-khahd. United . . . Only . . . Altogether . . . One. You are Eh-kahd, a United One. There is no one like You. How I praise Your name!

THE ONLY WISE GOD

אלהים

אחד לו הגדלה

Eh-lo-heem Eh-kahd Lo HaG'doo-lah

*Now unto the King eternal, immortal, invisible, the Only Wise God,
be honour and glory for ever and ever. Amen.*

I Timothy 1:17, KJV

156

Thank You dear God, that as long as I seek You, You give me help beyond my wildest dreams. Thank You that when I ask for wisdom, You give it. Eh-lo-heem Eh-kahd Lo HaG'doo-lah, the only wise God, thank You for Your help in all of my human circumstances. You are the plus to all of the minuses that are in my life. How I thank You for Your Wisdom—Past, Present and Future.

But You, O Sovereign LORD, deal well with me for Your name's sake; out of the goodness of Your love, deliver me. (Psalm 109:2)

OUR DWELLING PLACE

Mah-on

Lord, You have been our dwelling place throughout all generations.

Psalm 90:1, NIV

The same God who was the dwelling place for Moses, is the same God to me. When I am oppressed, when I am afraid, and when I don't know what to do, it is a comfort to run to You, Mah-on—Dwelling place—and rest there. Thank You that there is safety in the cleft of Your rock.

This is My name forever, the name by which I am to be remembered from generation to generation. (Exodus 3:15)

PLANT OF RENOWN

מטע לשם

Mah-tah L'Shaym

"And I will raise up for them a Plant of Renown, and they shall be no more consumed with hunger in the land, nor bear the shame of the heathen anymore."

Ezekiel 34:29, NKJV

160

You are the Plant of Renown, Mah-tah
L'Shaym, who supplies all that I will ever need.
The Everliving Plant, the Righteous Root,
Forever giving life, how I praise Your Name.

PRINCE OF PEACE

שר שלום

Sar Sha-lom

For unto us a child is born, to us a son is given, and the government will be on His shoulders. And He will be called . . . Prince of Peace.

Isaiah 9:6, NIV

When everything in my life seems uncontrollable, please help me to stop and remember that You are the Prince of Peace, Sar Sha-lom. You spoke, and the winds and the seas obeyed. You spoke "Peace, be still," and it was. Thank You for the peace that You speak into my life. I love You, Lord.

Let them know that You, whose name is the LORD - that You alone are the Most High over all the earth. (Psalm 83:18)

REDEEMER

Go-ah-lee

*May the words of my mouth and the meditation
of my heart be pleasing in Your sight, O LORD,
my Rock and my Redeemer.*

Psalm 19:14, NIV

164

There is none like You, O Lord. You lead me in paths of righteousness, for Your name's sake. Thank You for redeeming my life from the pit of hell. Thank You for paying a price that You did not have to, to redeem me, Go-ah-lee. My Redeemer is faithful and true and what You say, You will do. Your past faithfulness assures Your future promises will be kept. Thank You, Lord.

ROCK OF ISRAEL

אבן ישראל

Eh-ven Yis-rah-el

But his bow remained steady, his strong arms stayed limber, because of the hand of the Mighty One of Jacob, because of the Shepherd, the Rock of Israel, because of your father's God, who helps you.

Genesis 49:24, NIV

166

Dear God,

You are the only One who makes my hands strong. I shall not trust in my energy, brains, resources, contacts or anything else. I shall trust in You—Eh-ven Yis-rah-el, Rock of Israel; what a mighty defense You are. You have done it before for me and You will do it again.

Not to us, O LORD, not to us but to Your name be the glory because of Your love and faithfulness. (Psalm 115:1)

SAVIOR

מושיע

Mo-shee-ah

For I am the LORD, your God, the Holy One of Israel, your Savior.

Isaiah 43:3, NIV

168

Savior . . . Redeemer . . . LORD. You laid down
Your perfect sinless life so that I might be
saved. You took my place on the Cross; You
suffered, died, rose on the third day, and now
You sit at the Father's right hand.
Even though I shall never fully understand this,
I accept it by faith, Mo-shee-ah. May I live this
day as only You would live it. Help me to be a
vessel of love to all that I meet. Thank You, my
Savior, my deliverer, my Lord.

SHEPHERD

Ro-ee

The LORD is my shepherd, I shall not be in want.

Psalm 23:1, NIV

You are my Shepherd, my companion, Herdsman, Tender of the flock, my Ro-ee. Without You, Your people would perish. How I praise You, O Gentle Shepherd, for the blessed way that You lead me and guide me. You make me to lie down in green pastures; surely my cup overflows.

I will proclaim the name of the LORD. Oh, praise the greatness of our God! (Deuteuronomy 32:3)

SHEPHERD OF ISRAEL

רעה ישראל

Ro-eh Yis-rah-el

*Hear us, O Shepherd of Israel, You who lead
Joseph like a flock, You who sit enthroned
between the cherubim, shine forth.*

Psalm 80:1, NIV

To think that the One whose Presence dwelt between the cherubim comes to dwell with me, astounds me. Lord, how blessed am I to be led by the Shepherd of Israel, Ro-eh Yis-rah-el. Praises always to Your name.

SON OF DAVID

בֶּן דָּוִד

Ben Dah-veed

*As Yeshua Jesus went on from there, two blind men
followed Him, calling out, "Have mercy on us,
Son of David!"*

Matthew 9:27, NIV

174

Thank You Father for the mysteries of Your bloodline. It is a blessing to know the Son of David, Ben Dah-veed. May I be worthy to be called Your child; I thank You that it is not through my merit, but only through the Blood of Yeshua. Thank You for this royal inheritance.

Let the name of the LORD be praised, both now and forevermore. (Psalm 113:2)

SPIRIT OF GOD

רוּחַ אל

Roo-akh El

The Spirit of God has made me, the breath of the Almighty gives me life.

Job 33:4, NIV

Thank You, Spirit of God—Roo-akh El—for making me, shaping me, and molding me into the person that You want me to be. Thank You that Your Spirit is gentle, yet strong, to help me choose Your way. Not by might, nor by power, but only by Your Spirit is how I want to live. Thank You, Roo-akh El.

STRONG FORTRESS

צוּר

מָעוֹז

Tsoor Mah-oz

Turn Your ear to me, come quickly to my rescue; be my rock of refuge, a strong fortress to save me. Since You are my rock and my fortress, for the sake of Your name lead and guide me.

Psalm 31:2, NIV

O Lord, what a Rock You are, Tsoor Mah-oz. How I thank You for Your strength in my life. Be my strong rock, my Rock of the Ages. You are the defense of my life; how I praise You for that. Help me to live today with the calm assurance and peace of knowing that You are my strong fortress.

Therefore I will teach them—this time I will teach them My power and My might. Then they will know that My name is the LORD. (Jeremiah 16:21)

STRONG TOWER

מגדל

עז

Meeg-dahl Oz

The name of the LORD is a strong tower; the righteous run to it and are safe.

Proverbs 18:10, NIV

Lord, in times of distress, help me to run to You, O Strong Tower, Meeg-dahl Oz. You are my protection amid the storms of life. Thank You for Your sovereign protection and Your faithfulness.

SUN OF RIGHTEOUSNESS

שמש צדקה

Sheh-mesh Ts-dah-kah

But for you who revere My name, the Sun of Righteousness will rise with healing in its wings.

Malachi 4:2, NIV

182

How thankful I am to be able to look at the Sun of Righteousness, Sheh-mesh Ts-dah-kah. You are all the more glorious than I could ever hope for. Thank You for Your good plan for my life. It is a plan for my future and my hope. Thank You Lord.

In the night I remember Your name, O Lord, and I will keep Your law. (Psalm 119:55)

TRUE GOD

אמת אלהים

Eh-lo-heem Eh-met

*But the LORD is the true God; He is the living God,
the eternal King.*

Jeremiah 10:10, NIV

184

Thank You that You revealed Yourself to me—
Eh-lo-heem Eh-met, the True God. I desire no other
gods, but You, the True God. As all men search
for truth, how thankful I am to know You.

UPRIGHT ONE

Yah-shahr

The path of the righteous is level; O upright One,
You make the path of the righteous smooth.

Isaiah 26:7, NIV

186

O Father, O Upright One, Yah-shahr, You who dwell in righteousness, how I praise You. Thank You that everything that You do is perfect and right. There is no favoritism in You; just and true are all Your ways. I thank You for Your blessings in my life.

WONDERFUL

פלא

Peh-leh

For to us a son is born, to us a son is given, and the government will be on His shoulders. And He will be called Wonderful . . .

Isaiah 9:6, NIV

188

Wonderful—Peh-leh—A wonder; You. How thankful I am for the 'extraordinariness' of You! Your ways are higher than mine; how wonderful You are. May I live today with the inner assurance that the Wonderful God loves me.

In Judah, God is known; His name is great in Israel. (Psalm 76:1)

WORD OF GOD

דבר האלהים

D'vahr Ha'Ehlo-heem

*He is dressed in a robe dipped in blood, and
His name is the Word of God.*

Revelation 19:13, NIV

190

Just as You were in the beginning, You are the Word of God, D'vahr Ha'Ehlo-heem. Help me to get to know You more; day by day, by reading and meditating on Your Word, on You. How I love You, Lord.

YAH

Yah

*Sing to God, sing praises to His name; Extol Him who rides on the
clouds, By His name YAH, and rejoice before Him.*

Psalm 68:4, NKJV

192

Oh, YAH, may my praise be glorious to You! I
sing praises to Your name, YAH, for You reign
in the heavens; yet—You love me. Hallelujah!

*Glory in His holy name; let the hearts of those
who seek the LORD rejoice.* (Psalm 105:3)

YOU ARE THE GOD WHO SEES ME

אל ראי

El Ro-ee

She gave this name to the LORD who spoke to her;
You are the God who sees me, for she said 'I have
now seen the One who sees me."

Genesis 16:13, NIV

To know that I know You, and that You love me and see me is wonderful. You are the answer to all my questions, El Ro-ee. Thank You that I never have to search again. You fill my cup to overflowing. You are the One who sees me and loves me most. I praise Your name.

YOUR NAME

Sheem-kha

All the earth bows down to You; they sing praise to You,
they sing praise to Your name.

Psalm 66:4, NIV

Your Name is the Name Above all Names; how blessed am I to know Your name. How I praise Sheem-kha, Your Name. There is power in Your name, praise in Your name, healing in Your name, and help in Your name. There is everything I need—in Your name.

Praise the LORD. Praise, O servants of the LORD, praise the name of the LORD. (Psalm 113:1)

Appendix

Old Testament Names, Titles, and Descriptions of God

(Note: LORD = Jehovah, the self-Existent or Eternal; Lord = sovereign, lord, master, owner.)

A forgiving God — O LORD our God, You answered them; You were to Israel a forgiving God, though You punished their misdeeds. (Psalm 99:8)

A warrior — The LORD is a warrior; the LORD is His name. (Exodus 15:3)

Abounding in love — The LORD is compassionate and gracious, slow to anger, abounding in love. (Psalm 103:8)

Abounding in love and faithfulness — And He passed in front of Moses, proclaiming, "The LORD, the LORD, the compassionate and gracious God, slow to anger, abounding in love and faithfulness, maintaining love to thousands, and forgiving wickedness, rebellion and sin." (Exodus 34:6-7a)

Compassionate and gracious — The LORD is compassionate and gracious, slow to anger, abounding in love. (Psalm 103:8)

Creator — "Is this the way you repay the LORD, O foolish and unwise people? Is He not your Father, your Creator, who made you and formed you?" (Deuteronomy 32:6)

Creator of heaven and earth — Then Melchizedek king of Salem brought out bread and wine. He was priest of God Most High, and he blessed Abram, saying, "Blessed be Abram by God Most High, Creator of heaven and earth." (Genesis 14:18-19)

Creator of the ends of the earth — Do you not know? Have you not heard? The LORD is the everlasting God, the Creator of the ends of the earth. He will not grow tired or weary, and His understanding no one can fathom. (Isaiah 40:28)

Delights in those who fear Him — The LORD delights in those who fear Him, who put their hope in His unfailing love. (Psalm 147:10)

Eternal King — But the LORD is the true God; He is the living God, the eternal King. When He is angry, the earth trembles; the nations cannot endure His wrath. (Jeremiah 10:10)

Ever-present help —God is our refuge and strength, an ever-present help in trouble. (Psalm 46:1b)

Everlasting God — Do you not know? Have you not heard? The LORD is the everlasting God, the Creator of the ends of the earth. He will not grow tired or weary, and His understanding no one can fathom. (Isaiah 40:28)

Forgiving wickedness, rebellion, and sin — And he passed in front of Moses, proclaiming, "The LORD, the LORD, the compassionate and gracious God, slow to anger, abounding in love and faithfulness, maintaining love to thousands, and forgiving wickedness, rebellion and sin." (Exodus 34:6-7a)

God — In the beginning God created the heavens and the earth. (Genesis 1:1)

God Almighty — When Abram was ninety-nine years old, the LORD appeared to him and said, "I am God Almighty ; walk before Me and be blameless. (Genesis 17:1)

God Most High — My shield is God Most High, who saves the upright in heart. (Psalm 7:10)

God my Maker — "But no one says, 'Where is God my Maker, who gives songs in the night,'" (Job 35:10)

God my Savior — The LORD lives! Praise be to my Rock! Exalted be God my Savior! (Psalm 18:46)

Hebrew Names of God

God of Abraham — "If the God of my father, the God of Abraham and the Fear of Isaac, had not been with me, you would surely have sent me away empty-handed. But God has seen my hardship and the toil of my hands, and last night he rebuked you." (Genesis 31:42)

God of Abraham, Isaac, and Israel — At the time of sacrifice, the prophet Elijah stepped forward and prayed: "O LORD, God of Abraham, Isaac and Israel, let it be known today that You are God in Israel and that I am your servant and have done all these things at Your command." (1 King 18:36)

God of all flesh — Behold, I am the LORD, the God of all flesh: is there any thing too hard for Me? (Jeremiah 32:27, KJV)

God of all mankind — "I am the LORD, the God of all mankind. Is anything too hard for me?" (Jeremiah 32:27)

God of all the clans of Israel — "At that time," declares the LORD, "I will be the God of all the clans of Israel, and they will be My people." (Jeremiah 31:1)

God of all the earth — For your Maker is your husband—the LORD Almighty is His name—the Holy One of Israel is your Redeemer; He is called the God of all the earth. (Isaiah 54:5)

God of Bethel — I am the God of Bethel, where you anointed a pillar and where you made a vow to Me. Now leave this land at once and go back to your native land.'" (Genesis 31:13)

God of Daniel — "I issue a decree that in every part of my kingdom people must fear and reverence the God of Daniel. For He is the living God and He endures forever; His kingdom will not be destroyed, His dominion will never end." (Daniel 6:26)

God of Elijah — Then he took the cloak that had fallen from him and struck the water with it. "Where now is the LORD, the God of Elijah?" he asked. When he struck the water, it divided to the right and to the left, and he crossed over. (2 Kings 2:14)

God of glory — The voice of the LORD is over the waters; the God of glory thunders, the LORD thunders over the mighty waters. (Psalm 29:3)

God of gods — For the LORD your God is God of gods and Lord of lords, the great God, mighty and awesome, who shows no partiality and accepts no bribes. (Deuteronomy 10:17)

God of heaven — "This is what Cyrus king of Persia says: "'The LORD, the God of heaven, has given me all the kingdoms of the earth and He has appointed me to build a temple for Him at Jerusalem in Judah.'" (2 Chronicles 36:23)

God of heaven and God of earth — "I want you to swear by the LORD, the God of heaven and the God of earth, that you will not get a wife for my son from the daughters of the Canaanites, among whom I am living." (Genesis 24:3)

God of hosts — Turn us again, O God of hosts, and cause Thy face to shine; and we shall be saved. (Psalm 80:7, KJV)

God of Isaac — There above it stood the LORD, and He said: "I am the LORD, the God of your father Abraham and the God of Isaac. I will give you and your descendants the land on which you are lying." (Genesis 28:13)

God of Israel — O my people, crushed on the threshing floor, I tell you what I have heard from the LORD Almighty, from the God of Israel. (Isaiah 21:10)

God of Jacob — These are the last words of David: "The oracle of David son of Jesse, the oracle of the man exalted by the Most High, the man anointed by the God of Jacob, Israel's singer of songs" (2 Samuel 23:1)

God of Jerusalem — They spoke about the God of Jerusalem as they did about the gods of the other peoples of the world—the work of men's hands. (2 Chronicles 32:19)

God of Jeshurun — "There is no one like the God of Jeshurun, who rides on the heavens to help you and on the clouds in His majesty." (Deuteronomy 33:26)

God of justice — Yet the LORD longs to be gracious to you; He rises to show you compassion. For the LORD is a God of justice. Blessed are all who wait for Him! (Isaiah 30:18)

God of my life — By day the LORD directs his love, at night His song is with me— a prayer to the God of my life. (Psalm 42:8)

God of Nahor — "May the God of Abraham and the God of Nahor, the God of their father, judge between us." So Jacob took an oath in the name of the Fear of his father Isaac. (Genesis 31:53)

God of retribution — A destroyer will come against Babylon; her warriors will be captured, and their bows will be broken. For the LORD is a God of retribution; He will repay in full. (Jeremiah 51:56)

God of Shadrach, Meshach and Abednego — Then Nebuchadnezzar said, "Praise be to the God of Shadrach, Meshach and Abednego, who has sent His angel and rescued His servants! They trusted in Him and defied the king's command and were willing to give up their lives rather than serve or worship any god except their own God." (Daniel 3:28)

God of Shem — He also said, "Blessed be the LORD, the God of Shem! May Canaan be the slave of Shem." (Genesis 9:26)

God of the armies of Israel — David said to the Philistine, "You come against me with sword and spear and javelin, but I come against you in the name of the LORD Almighty, the God of the armies of Israel, whom you have defied." (1 Samuel 17:45)

God of the spirits of all mankind — But Moses and Aaron fell facedown and cried out, "O God, God of the spirits of all mankind, will you be angry with the entire assembly when only one man sins?" (Numbers 16:22)

God of truth — Into your hands I commit my spirit; redeem me, O LORD, the God of truth. (Psalm 31:5)

God of your father David — "Go back and tell Hezekiah, the leader of my people, 'This is what the LORD, the God of your father David, says: I have heard your prayer and seen your tears; I will heal you. On the third day from now you will go up to the temple of the LORD." (2 Kings 20:5)

God of your fathers — God also said to Moses, "Say to the Israelites, 'The LORD, the God of your fathers—the God of Abraham, the God of Isaac and the God of Jacob—has sent me to you.' This is My name forever, the name by which I am to be remembered from generation to generation. (Exodus 3:15)

God over all the kingdoms of the earth — And Hezekiah prayed to the LORD: "O LORD, God of Israel, enthroned between the cherubim, you alone are God over all the kingdoms of the earth. You have made heaven and earth." (2 Kings 19:15)

God the King — *From a psalm of praise of David*. I will exalt you, my God the King; I will praise your name for ever and ever. (Psalm 145:1)

God the LORD — This is what God the LORD says—-He who created the heavens and stretched them out, who spread out the earth and all that comes out of it, who gives breath to its people, and life to those who walk on it. (Isaiah 42:5)

God who avenges — O LORD, the God who avenges, O God who avenges, shine forth. (Psalm 94:1)

God who performs miracles — You are the God who performs miracles; you display your power among the peoples. (Psalm 77:14)

God who provides — Abraham answered, "God himself will provide the lamb for the burnt offering, my son." And the two of them went on together. (Genesis 22:8)

Great and awesome God — Then I said: "O LORD, God of heaven, the great and awesome God, who keeps his covenant of love with those who love him and obey his commands," (Nehemiah 1:4)

Great and mighty in power — Great is our Lord and mighty in power; His understanding has no limit. (Psalm 147:5)

Heals the brokenhearted — He heals the brokenhearted and binds up their wounds. (Psalm 147:3)

Holy One of Israel — Our Redeemer—the LORD Almighty is His name—is the Holy One of Israel. (Isaiah 47:4)

Hope of their fathers — "Whoever found them devoured them; their enemies said, 'We are not guilty, for they sinned against the LORD, their true pasture, the LORD, the hope of their fathers.'" (Jeremiah 50:7)

Horn of my salvation — The LORD is my rock, my fortress and my deliverer; my God is my rock, in whom I take refuge. He is my shield and the horn of my salvation, my stronghold. (Psalm 18:2)

I AM — God said to Moses, "I AM WHO I AM. This is what you are to say to the Israelites: 'I AM has sent me to you.'" (Exodus 3:14)

I AM WHO I AM — God said to Moses, "I AM WHO I AM. This is what you are to say to the Israelites: 'I AM has sent me to you.'" (Exodus 3:14)

Israel's Creator — "I am the LORD, your Holy One, Israel's Creator, your King." (Isaiah 43:15)

Israel's King and Redeemer — "This is what the LORD says— Israel's King and Redeemer, the LORD Almighty: I am the first and I am the last; apart from Me there is no God." (Isaiah 44:6)

Jacob's King — "Present your case," says the LORD. "Set forth your arguments," says Jacob's King. (Isaiah 41:21)

Judge — "I have not wronged you, but you are doing me wrong by waging war against me. Let the LORD, the Judge, decide the dispute this day between the Israelites and the Ammonites." (Judges 11:27)

Judge of all the earth — "Far be it from you to do such a thing—to kill the righteous with the wicked, treating the righteous and the wicked alike. Far be it from you! Will not the Judge of all the earth do right?" (Genesis 18:25)

King of all the earth — For God is the King of all the earth; sing to him a psalm of praise. (Psalm 47:7)

King of glory — Lift up your heads, O you gates; be lifted up, you ancient doors, that the King of glory may come in. (Psalm 24:7)

King of heaven — Now I, Nebuchadnezzar, praise and exalt and glorify the King of heaven, because everything he does is right and all His ways are just. And those who walk in pride He is able to humble. (Daniel 4:37)

King of the nations — Who should not revere you, O King of the nations? This is Your due. Among all the wise men of the nations and in all their kingdoms, there is no one like You. (Jeremiah 10:7)

Living God — For what mortal man has ever heard the voice of the living God speaking out of fire, as we have, and survived? (Deuteronomy 5:26)

LORD — The LORD said, "Go out and stand on the mountain in the presence of the LORD, for the LORD is about to pass by." Then a great and powerful wind tore the mountains apart and shattered the rocks before the LORD, but the LORD was not in the wind. After the wind there was an earthquake, but the LORD was not in the earthquake. (1 King 19:11)

LORD Almighty — He and all his men set out from Baalah of Judah to bring up from there the ark of God, which is called by the Name, the name of the LORD Almighty, who is enthroned between the cherubim that are on the ark. (2 Samuel 6:2)

LORD Almighty, the God of Israel — "Therefore, this is what the LORD Almighty, the God of Israel, says: I am determined to bring disaster on you and to destroy all Judah." (Jeremiah 44:11)

LORD Almighty, who dwells on Mount Zion — Here am I, and the children the LORD has given me. We are signs and symbols in Israel from the LORD Almighty, who dwells on Mount Zion. (Isaiah 8:18)

LORD God Almighty — He replied, "I have been very zealous for the LORD God Almighty. The Israelites have rejected Your covenant, broken down your altars, and put Your prophets to death with the sword. I am the only one left, and now they are trying to kill me too." (1 King 19:10)

LORD God of Israel — "I hate divorce," says the LORD God of Israel, "and I hate a man's covering himself with violence as well as with his garment," says the LORD Almighty. So guard yourself in your spirit, and do not break faith." (Malachi 2:16)

LORD God of the Hebrews — And they shall hearken to thy voice: and thou shalt come, thou and the elders of Israel, unto the king of Egypt, and

214

ye shall say unto him, The LORD God of the Hebrews hath met with us: and now let us go, we beseech thee, three days' journey into the wilderness, that we may sacrifice to the LORD our God. (Exodus 3:18)

LORD my God — "See, I have taught you decrees and laws as the LORD my God commanded me, so that you may follow them in the land you are entering to take possession of it." (Deuteronomy 4:5)

Lord of all the earth — "See, the ark of the covenant of the Lord of all the earth will go into the Jordan ahead of you." (Joshua 3:11)

Lord of heaven — "Instead, you have set yourself up against the Lord of heaven. You had the goblets from His temple brought to you, and you and your nobles, your wives and your concubines drank wine from them. You praised the gods of silver and gold, of bronze, iron, wood and stone, which cannot see or hear or understand. But you did not honor the God who holds in his hand your life and all your ways." (Daniel 5:23)

Lord of kings — The king said to Daniel, "Surely your God is the God of gods and the Lord of kings and a revealer of mysteries, for you were able to reveal this mystery." (Daniel 2:47)

Lord of lords — For the LORD your God is God of gods and Lord of lords, the great God, mighty and awesome, who shows no partiality and accepts no bribes. (Deuteronomy 10:17)

Lord of the whole world — The angel answered me, "These are the four spirits of heaven, going out from standing in the presence of the Lord of the whole world." (Zechariah 6:5)

LORD our God — And the people said to Joshua, "We will serve the LORD our God and obey him." (Joshua 24:24)

LORD our Maker — Come, let us bow down in worship, let us kneel before the LORD our Maker. (Psalm 95:6)

LORD your God — "For I am the LORD your God, who churns up the sea so that its waves roar—the LORD Almighty is His name." (Isaiah 51:15)

LORD your Maker — "that you forget the LORD your Maker, who stretched out the heavens and laid the foundations of the earth, that you live in constant terror every day because of the wrath of the oppressor, who is bent on destruction? For where is the wrath of the oppressor?" (Isaiah 51:13)

LORD your Redeemer — "In a surge of anger I hid my face from you for a moment, but with everlasting kindness I will have compassion on you," says the LORD your Redeemer. (Isaiah 54:8)

LORD, who heals you — He said, "If you listen carefully to the voice of the LORD your God and do what is right in His eyes, if you pay attention to His commands and keep all His decrees, I will not bring on you any of the diseases I brought on the Egyptians, for I am the LORD, who heals you." (Exodus 15:26)

LORD, who makes you holy — "Say to the Israelites, 'You must observe my Sabbaths. This will be a sign between Me and you for the generations to come, so you may know that I am the LORD, who makes you holy. (Exodus 31:13)

Maintaining love to thousands — And he passed in front of Moses, proclaiming, "The LORD, the LORD, the compassionate and gracious

God, slow to anger, abounding in love and faithfulness, maintaining love to thousands, and forgiving wickedness, rebellion and sin." (Exodus 34:6-7a)

Maker of all things — He who is the Portion of Jacob is not like these, for He is the Maker of all things, including Israel, the tribe of his inheritance—the LORD Almighty is his name. (Jeremiah 10:16)

Mighty and awesome — For the LORD your God is God of gods and Lord of lords, the great God, mighty and awesome, who shows no partiality and accepts no bribes. (Deuteronomy 10:17)

Mighty One of Israel — Therefore the Lord, the LORD Almighty, the Mighty One of Israel, declares: "Ah, I will get relief from My foes and avenge myself on My enemies. (Isaiah 1:24)

Mighty One of Jacob — But his bow remained steady, his strong arms stayed limber, because of the hand of the Mighty One of Jacob, because of the Shepherd, the Rock of Israel. (Genesis 49:24)

Hebrew Names of God

Most High — The LORD thundered from heaven; the voice of the Most High resounded. (Psalm 18:13)

My deliverer — The LORD is my rock, my fortress and my deliverer; my God is my rock, in whom I take refuge. He is my shield and the horn of my salvation, my stronghold. (Psalm 18:2)

My fortress — The LORD is my rock, my fortress and my deliverer; my God is my rock, in whom I take refuge. He is my shield and the horn of my salvation, my stronghold. (Psalm 18:2)

My God — With your help I can advance against a troop; with my God I can scale a wall. (2 Samuel 22:30)

My Rock — The LORD lives! Praise be to my Rock! Exalted be God my Savior! (Psalm 18:46)

My Salvation — The LORD is my strength and my song; He has become my salvation. He is my God, and I will praise Him, my father's God, and I will exalt Him. (Exodus 15:2)

My Shield — The LORD is my rock, my fortress and my deliverer; my God is my rock, in whom I take refuge. He is my shield and the horn of my salvation, my stronghold. (Psalm 18:2)

My Strength and my Song — The LORD is my strength and my song; He has become my salvation. He is my God, and I will praise Him, my father's God, and I will exalt Him. (Exodus 15:2)

Our Father — "But you are our Father, though Abraham does not know us or Israel acknowledge us; you, O LORD, are our Father, our Redeemer from of old is Your name." (Isaiah 63:16)

Our God for ever and ever — For this God is our God for ever and ever; He will be our guide even to the end. (Psalm 48:14)

Our Guide — For this God is our God for ever and ever; He will be our guide even to the end. (Psalm 48:14)

Our Judge — For the LORD is our judge, the LORD is our lawgiver, the LORD is our king; it is He who will save us. (Isaiah 33:22)

Our King — For the LORD is our judge, the LORD is our lawgiver, the LORD is our king; it is He who will save us. (Isaiah 33:22)

Our Lawgiver — For the LORD is our judge, the LORD is our lawgiver, the LORD is our king; it is He who will save us. (Isaiah 33:2)

Our Redeemer — Our Redeemer—the LORD Almighty is His name—is the Holy One of Israel. (Isaiah 47:4)

Refuge and Strength — God is our refuge and strength, an ever-present help in trouble. (Psalm 46:1b)

Refuge for the needy — You have been a refuge for the poor, a refuge for the needy in his distress, a shelter from the storm and a shade from the heat. (Isaiah 25:4)

Refuge for the poor — You have been a refuge for the poor, a refuge for the needy in his distress, a shelter from the storm and a shade from the heat. (Isaiah 25:4)

Righteous Judge — God is a righteous judge, a God who expresses His wrath every day. (Psalm 7:11)

Shade from the heat — You have been a refuge for the poor, a refuge for the needy in his distress, a shelter from the storm and a shade from the heat. (Isaiah 25:4)

Shelter from the storm — You have been a refuge for the poor, a refuge for the needy in his distress, a shelter from the storm and a shade from the heat. (Isaiah 25:4)

Shield — As for God, His way is perfect; the word of the LORD is flawless. He is a shield for all who take refuge in Him. (Psalm 18:30)

Shield and Helper — Blessed are you, O Israel! Who is like you, a people saved by the LORD? He is your shield and helper and your glorious sword. Your enemies will cower before you, and you will trample down their high places. (Deuteronomy 33:29)

Slow to anger — The LORD is compassionate and gracious, slow to anger, abounding in love. (Psalm 103:8)

Sovereign LORD — This is what the Sovereign LORD says: "See, I will beckon to the Gentiles, I will lift up My banner to the peoples;

they will bring your sons in their arms and carry your daughters on their shoulders." (Isaiah 49:22)

Sovereign LORD Almighty — The LORD has opened his arsenal and brought out the weapons of His wrath, for the Sovereign LORD Almighty has work to do in the land of the Babylonians. (Jeremiah 50:25)

Stronghold — The LORD is my rock, my fortress and my deliverer; my God is my rock, in whom I take refuge. He is my shield and the horn of my salvation, my stronghold. (Psalm 18:2)

Sun and Shield — For the LORD God is a sun and shield; the LORD bestows favor and honor; no good thing does He withhold from those whose walk is blameless. (Psalm 84:11)

Sustains the humble — The LORD sustains the humble but casts the wicked to the ground. (Psalm 147:6)

The Almighty — because of your father's God, who helps you, because of the Almighty, who blesses you with blessings of the heavens above, blessings of the deep that lies below, blessings of the breast and womb. (Genesis 49:25)

The fear of Isaac — "If the God of my father, the God of Abraham and the Fear of Isaac, had not been with me, you would surely have sent me away empty-handed. But God has seen my hardship and the toil of my hands, and last night he rebuked you." (Genesis 31:42)

The first and the last — "This is what the LORD says—Israel's King and Redeemer, the LORD Almighty: I am the first and I am the last; apart from Me there is no God." (Isaiah 44:6)

The God of Abraham, the God of Isaac, and the God of Jacob — God also said to Moses, "Say to the Israelites, 'The LORD, the God of your fathers—the God of Abraham, the God of Isaac, and the God of Jacob—has sent me to you.' This is My name forever, the name by which I am to be remembered from generation to generation. (Exodus 3:15)

The Great God — For the LORD your God is God of gods and Lord of lords, the great God, mighty and awesome, who shows no partiality and accepts no bribes. (Deuteronomy 10:17)

The Great King — It is beautiful in its loftiness, the joy of the whole earth. Like the utmost heights of Zaphon is Mount Zion, the city of the Great King. (Psalm 48:2)

The King of Israel — The LORD has taken away your punishment, he has turned back your enemy. The LORD, the King of Israel, is with you; never again will you fear any harm. (Zephaniah 3:15)

The Lord Almighty — He who is the Portion of Jacob is not like these, for He is the Maker of all things, including Israel, the tribe of his inheritance—the LORD Almighty is His name. (Jeremiah 10:16)

The LORD is my Banner — Moses built an altar and called it The LORD is my Banner. (Exodus 17:15)

The LORD is Peace — So Gideon built an altar to the LORD there and called it The LORD is Peace. To this day it stands in Ophrah of the Abiezrites. (Judges 6:24)

The LORD Will Provide — So Abraham called that place The LORD Will Provide. And to this day it is said, "On the mountain of the LORD it will be provided." (Genesis 22:14)

The Rock — For who is God besides the LORD? And who is the Rock except our God? (Psalm 18:31)

The Rock of Israel — But his bow remained steady, his strong arms stayed limber, because of the hand of the Mighty One of Jacob, because of the Shepherd, the Rock of Israel, (Genesis 49:24)

The Shepherd — But his bow remained steady, his strong arms stayed limber, because of the hand of the Mighty One of Jacob, because of the Shepherd, the Rock of Israel, (Genesis 49:24)

True God — But the LORD is the true God; He is the living God, the eternal King. When He is angry, the earth trembles; the nations cannot endure His wrath. (Jeremiah 10:10)

Understanding has no limit — Great is our Lord and mighty in power; His understanding has no limit. (Psalm 147:5)

Wonderful in counsel and magnificent in wisdom — All this also comes from the LORD Almighty, wonderful in counsel and magnificent in wisdom.

(Isaiah 28:29)

Your everlasting light — "The sun will no more be your light by day, nor will the brightness of the moon shine on you, for the LORD will be your everlasting light, and your God will be your glory." (Isaiah 60:19)

Your glory — "The sun will no more be your light by day, nor will the brightness of the moon shine on you, for the LORD will be your everlasting light, and your God will be your glory." (Isaiah 60:19)

Your God — I will establish my covenant as an everlasting covenant between Me and you and your descendants after you for the generations to come, to be your God and the God of your descendants after you. (Genesis 17:7)

Your Holy One — "I am the LORD, your Holy One, Israel's Creator, your King." (Isaiah 43:15)

Your Husband — For your Maker is your husband—the LORD Almighty is His name—the Holy One of Israel is your Redeemer; He is called the God of all the earth. (Isaiah 54:5)

Your King — "I am the LORD, your Holy One, Israel's Creator, your King." (Isaiah 43:15)

Your Maker — For your Maker is your husband—the LORD Almighty is His name—the Holy One of Israel is your Redeemer; He is called the God of all the earth. (Isaiah 54:5)

Your Redeemer — "Do not be afraid, O worm Jacob, O little Israel, for I Myself will help you," declares the LORD, your Redeemer, the Holy One of Israel." (Isaiah 41:14)

Your Savior — "I will make your oppressors eat their own flesh; they will be drunk on their own blood, as with wine. Then all mankind will know that I, the LORD, am your Savior, your Redeemer, the Mighty One of Jacob." (Isaiah 49:26)

Hebrew Names of God

PRONUNCIATION GUIDE TO TRANSLITERATION

A .... Short A as in Dog or Ahhhhh
A .... Long A as in Say or Day
E .... Short E as in Tent or Kept
E .... Long E as in Sheep or Keep
I .... Long I as in Child or Wild
O .... Long O as in Old or Snow
O .... O as in Goo or Shoe
Kh ..... Gutteral sound as in clearing the throat
       There is no soft 'g' or 'j' sound in Hebrew
       All G's are hard, as in guess or guest